A SHETLAND PATTERN BOOK

A SHETLAND PATTERN BOOK

Knitting designs
selected and edited by
MARY SMITH
MAGGIE LIDDLE

The Shetland Times Ltd
Lerwick
1992

© Mary Smith & Maggie Liddle, 1992

ISBN: 0 900662 80 8

First edition 1979
Eleventh (revised) edition 1992

Cover design by John Birtle

British Library Cataloguing-in-Publication Data

A catalogue record for this book is
available from the British Library

Printed and published by
The Shetland Times Ltd.,
Lerwick, Shetland, Scotland

CONTENTS

ACKNOWLEDGEMENTS

We selected these patterns from our own collections with additional help from the pattern books of Mrs Betty Twatt of Lerwick and the late Miss Agnes Smith of South Whiteness.

The photography was by John Birtle, featuring knitting by Nellie Leask of Lerwick.

We would like to mention David and Alex for their comments, useful and otherwise.

To all the above — thank you.

1

DEDICATION

To Maud and her friends who made this book possible.

ABOUT THE AUTHORS

Mary Smith has spent much of her life in Shetland. She ran a successful knitwear business — The Knitting Machine — and during a nine-year stay in Edinburgh set up and ran 'Johnny Notions' — a gift shop. While there she worked as Exhibition Organiser for the Scottish Craft Centre and wrote a second book on knitting — *A Shetland Knitter's Notebook*. She has recently returned to Shetland.

Maggie Liddle grew up in Caithness and went to Edinburgh College of Art where she specialised in tapestry weaving. She continues to do her own artwork, teaches art and design at the Anderson High School in Lerwick and is a tutor with the Open College of the Arts.

INTRODUCTION

One of the many objects found in the Shetland home is a school graph book which contains the family's collection of knitting patterns, used as the basis for decoration of garments. As knitting traditions change, we thought a Shetland Pattern Book should be produced in the form of a practical textbook. The following selection is personal and subjective. We have, however, tried to cover as wide a range as possible. From this the knitter can make her own combinations and permutations and we are simply providing a reference and starting point.

The inspiration for these patterns comes from many sources, natural and formal, used in combination. There are established symbols, such as the Greek key, natural forms — waves, stars and flowers, and geometric designs, sometimes taken from contemporary fabrics and artifacts (like the wife whose jumper matched her lino). Patterns are modified to suit the garment and the wearer — for instance, anchors for a sailor.

The more traditional items were knitted in natural colours: fawn, moorit (a light brown coloured sheep, native to Shetland), grey, white and Shetland Black (very dark brown). With modern dyeing processes, however, the colour choice is wide and the possibilities endless.

We have enjoyed arranging this book. We hope you will enjoy using it.

Mary Smith
Maggie Liddle
1979

GARMENTS AND IDEAS

In the Shetland Islands knitters select various patterns for use in particular garments from their own collections. This book will enable you to do the same. We do not include specific garment instructions in our book. The patterns may be introduced to any of your favourite knitting designs or those obtainable in leaflet form from most wool shops. Although 2-ply Shetland wool is used most often (equivalent to normal 4-ply yarn), the patterns can be made up in wool of various thicknesses and textures. As two strands are used in each row a double thickness is achieved.

Individuality is the keynote. Four ladies given the same set of patterns and wool colours would probably produce four very different results! There are conventions but not rules. Woollen clothes do not have to be boring. Jumpers must keep you warm in winter and they can also be attractive and decorative. Fine lace yarn makes beautiful evening clothes; why not incorporate a Fair Isle border on the skirt of an evening dress?

Over the last few years fashion designers have been returning to natural fibres and ethnic designs. Why not design your own clothing using these traditional patterns, or take it a step further and design your own patterns? Shetland patterns can also be incorporated into an infinite number of knitted goods for use throughout the home — cushion covers, wall-hangings, bedspreads or an enormous woolly jumper to encase your favourite armchair. We hope our pattern book will also be of use to non-knitters who could work the designs into rugs and tapestries.

Fig. 1

KNITTING IMPLEMENTS AND ACCESSORIES

A special feature of Shetland knitwear is the fact that garments are seamless. The needles, or 'wires' as they are usually called in Shetland, are pointed at both ends; three are used simultaneously, one for the front, one for the back and a working wire. To achieve a seamless effect a circular knitting needle can be substituted or four needles used as when knitting socks. The needles are longer than average and until recently were made of steel which was less easy to bend. Shoulder seams are joined by grafting.

Knitting sheathes were once common in the Scottish and English border counties. The Shetland knitting belt has developed from these. It is made of leather with the pad stuffed full of horse-hair. The belt is fastened around the knitter's waist with the pad on the right side; the holes in this pad secure one end of the needle.

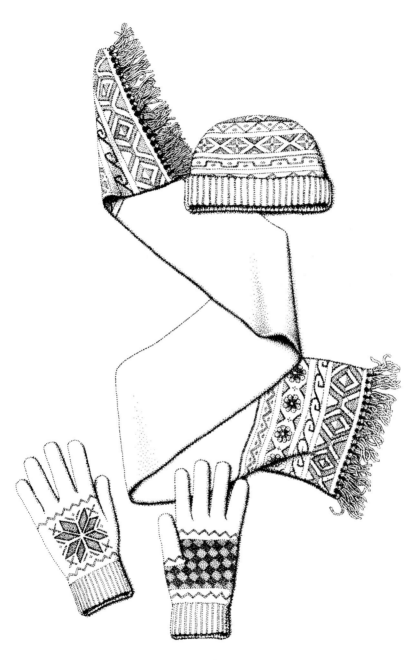

Fig. 2

9

GARMENT CARE

When the garment is finished and taken 'off the wires' it has to be washed and dressed. To dress a garment means to stretch it when wet over a frame. These frames are usually of wood and often home-made. Jumper-boards or 'woolly horses' are found in nearly every home. They are usually adjustable and used for the jumpers of all the family, although sometimes a simpler frame is made which is a set size and used only for garments measuring that particular size (see fig. 3).

Hats can be stretched over pudding basins, berets on dinner plates and special boards are usually made for scarves, gloves, mitts and socks (see fig. 4). When a new shaped garment comes into fashion a board is often made for the purpose.

A thread is stitched around neck ribs and around the ribs of berets and pulled tightly to give a neat tight rib. After removing jumpers from the board the rib is loose and needs to be shaped. The ribs can be pressed with a hot iron and damp cloth or held over the steam from a boiling kettle.

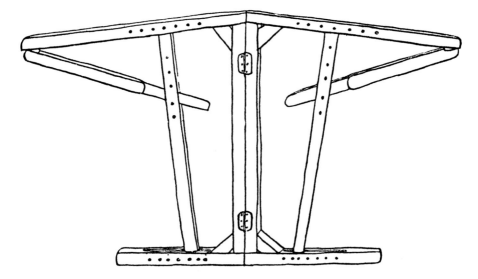

Woolly Horse

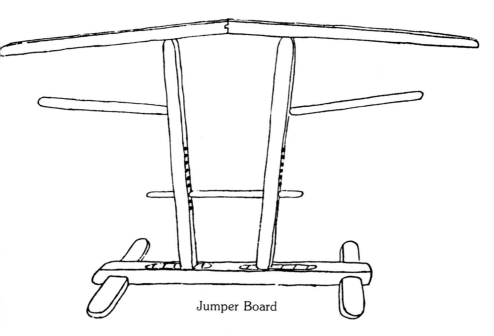

Jumper Board

Fig.3

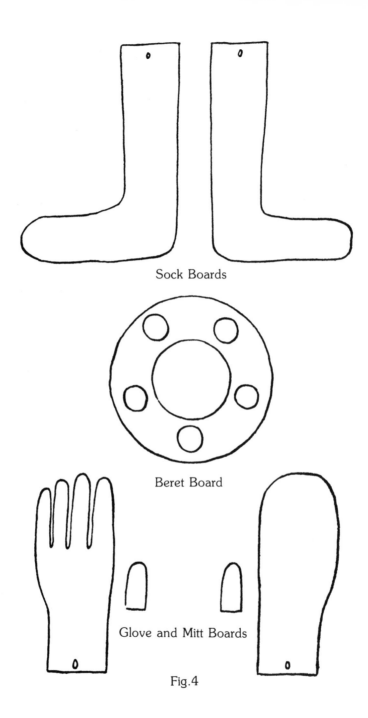

Sock Boards

Beret Board

Glove and Mitt Boards

Fig.4

12

NOTES ON THE PATTERNS

The following patterns increase in size from two row borders to large Norwegian Stars. In the very old garments smaller patterns predominate (see fig. 1), but today the Norwegian Star appears on everything, gloves to allovers (fig. 2), and it has thus been included alongside the more traditional 'Fair Isle' patterns. From these graphs the knitter chooses appropriate patterns to combine for her garment.

Every knitter shades and colours patterns individually but there are certain conventions, for instance, no more than two colours in one row. Small nine row patterns are usually shaded with changes every two rows and a contrasting colour in the centre, but often the pattern itself suggests where the colour should change.

The following notes are not rigid rules, only suggestions and thoughts, with scope for your own imagination. Border patterns have many applications. They can be used to fill an entire garment, particularly small articles; to separate larger patterns, to decorate small pieces — bags, pin-cushions, to frame or edge knitting, for a child's or beginner's sampler.

Each row of pattern 1h may be knitted in a different colour on the same background to give depth or to unite a colour scheme. A scallop effect is achieved with pattern 2i if the same colour is used to knit 2i at the edge of a yoke as is used for the background of the yoke. Pattern 3e can be built up and used to give shaded diamonds, which are frequently used to separate larger patterns on allover jumpers and scarves. Different arrangements of colour in 5g give a variety of effect from shaded blocks to a pseudo tartan check.

Nine, 11 and 13 row patterns are used very widely in all types of knitting and are particularly suitable for children's wear, to trim necks and cuffs, gloves and on hats and berets. Smaller patterns in combination with crosses are said to be the traditional Fair Isle designs.

There are very few ten row patterns. Most patterns are of uneven numbers to provide a single central row. When wool was hand-dyed this central row could be picked out in a rare or expensive colour.

Colours are often changed according to the shape of the pattern, as in 7b where the pattern is made up of three row blocks. Do not be deterred by the simplicity of such patterns. The shading of the background in some patterns, such as 8d, can be as important as the pattern itself. In 8d the patterns can be worked throughout in one colour and all colour changes made on the background shades.

Pattern 11b is popular for children's allovers. The central O-shape can be changed to an X on alternate pattern bands and by using alternating colours an unusual stripe-effect can be made.

15d is one of the most well used and most versatile patterns and seems to occur on every kind of garment, socks to night caps. 15, 17 and

19 row patterns are used mostly on yokes, allover jumpers and scarves or centred on the backs of gloves, on ski-caps and as borders on machine-made scarves and jumpers. Small borders are used in addition to these patterns to add width or emphasise the design.

Norwegian stars are used for the back of gloves and mitts, the palm is knitted with a simple pattern to carry the colours. The work of a lady who specialises in knitting gloves (the best are said to come from Cunningsburgh) can often be identified by her particular palm pattern.

On yoke jumpers a tree is worked in conjunction with the star, and decreasing is done on the stitches on either side of the tree where it starts to taper. Chains and anchors may also be used for the same purpose.

By using simple patterns to link up Norwegian stars a continuous allover garment can be made.

Two colour knitting often in black and white gives a snowflake effect, but some knitters use upwards of twenty colours in one garment. Most knitters in the islands keep all left-over wool from previous work and when a new garment is being designed these scraps and balls of yarn are often used.

Continuous patterns are especially suitable for two colour knitting and in recent years are used on knitting machines which can cope with limited Fair Isle patterns. Novelty patterns were popular for children's clothes but are not so common nowadays. A pattern such as 39c would be used to decorate the neckline of a child's jumper. The running men of 41c might appear on a matching jumper and hat set.

Everyday items — teapots or older, traditional crofthouse utensils like peat tongs and cooking pots — become decorative if somewhat unusual designs.

Many novelty designs are quite patriotic and even royalist — crowns, flags and thistles.

INDEX TO PATTERNS

Border Patterns

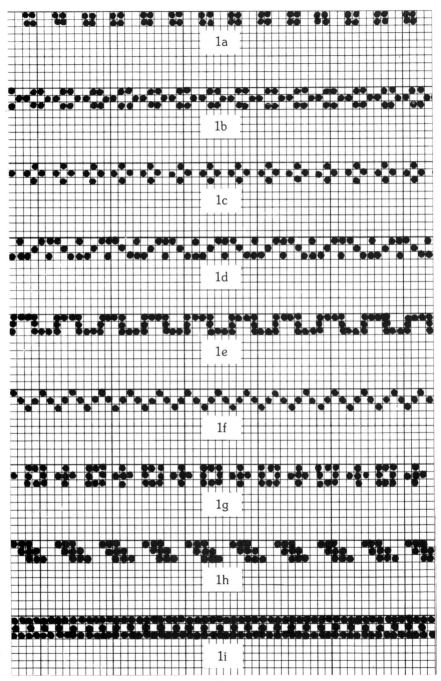

1a

1b

1c

1d

1e

1f

1g

1h

1i

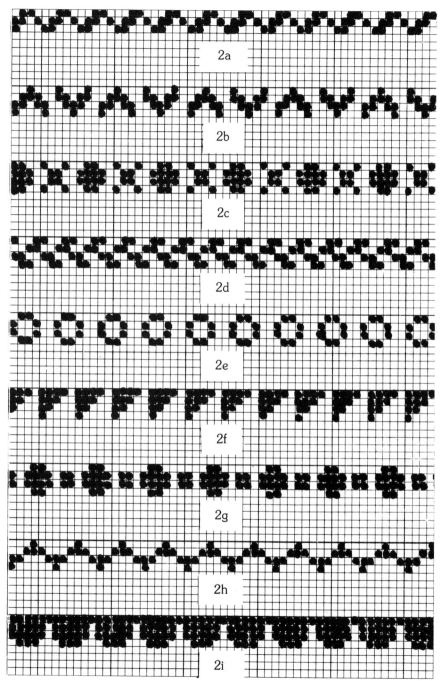

2a

2b

2c

2d

2e

2f

2g

2h

2i

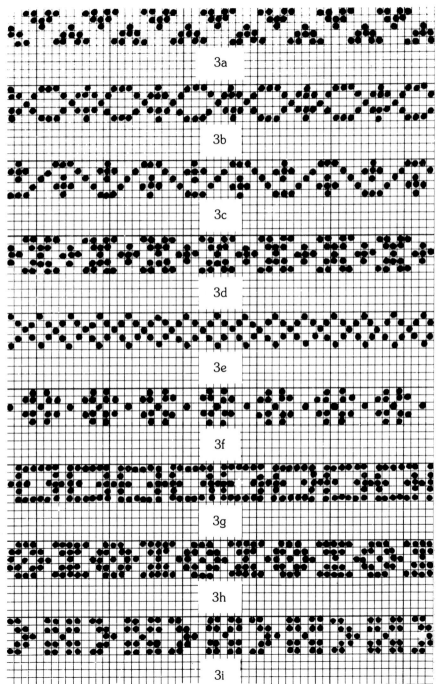

3a

3b

3c

3d

3e

3f

3g

3h

3i

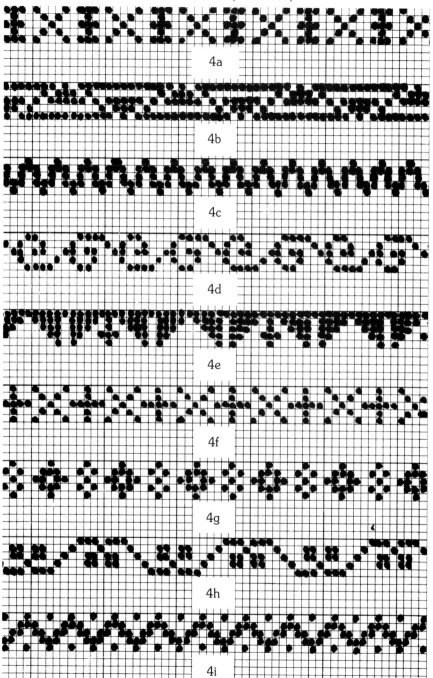

4a

4b

4c

4d

4e

4f

4g

4h

4i

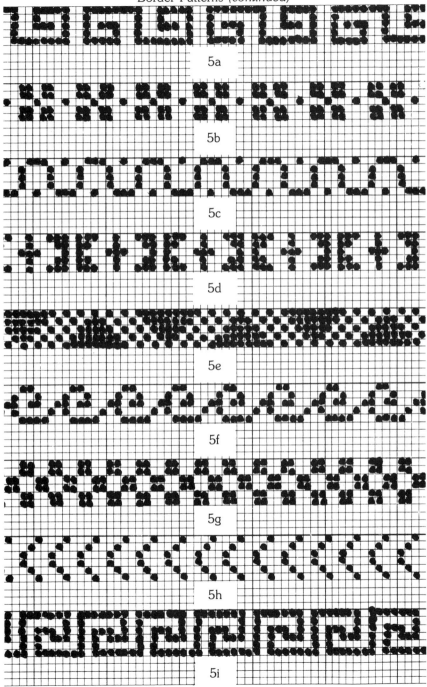

5a

5b

5c

5d

5e

5f

5g

5h

5i

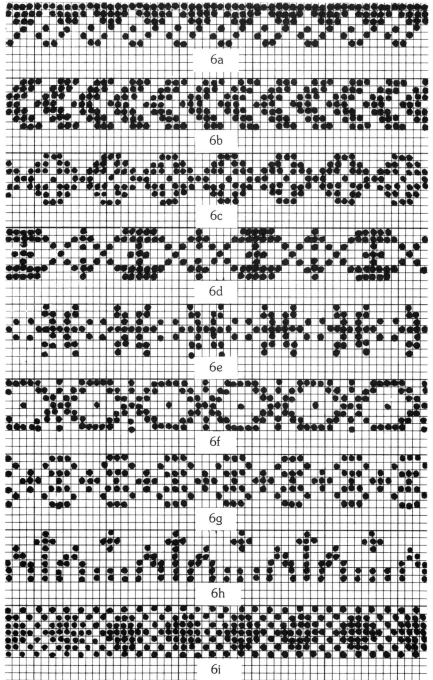

6a

6b

6c

6d

6e

6f

6g

6h

6i

9 Row Patterns

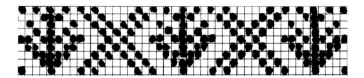

7a

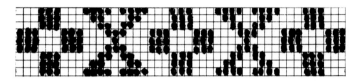

7b

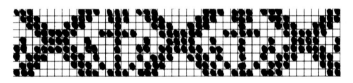

7c

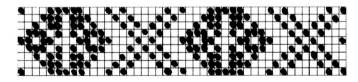

7d

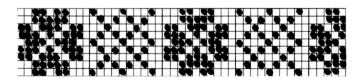

7e

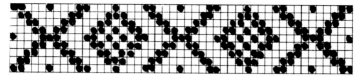

8a

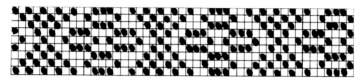

8b

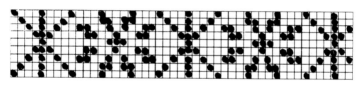

8c

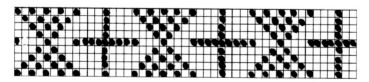

8d

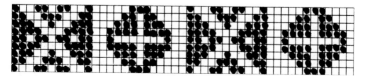

8e

9 Row Patterns *(continued)*

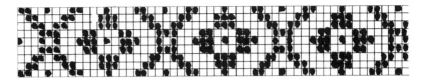

9a

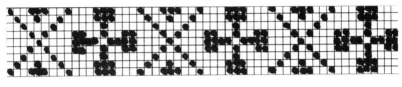

9b

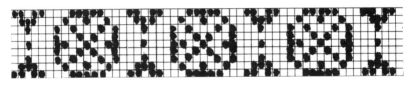

9c

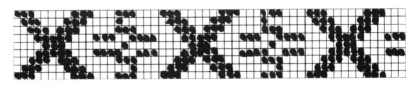

9d

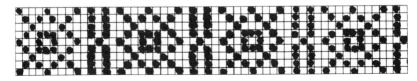

9e

9 Row Patterns *(continued)*

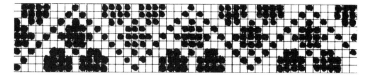

10a

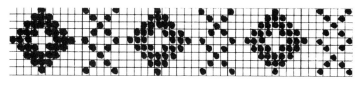

10b

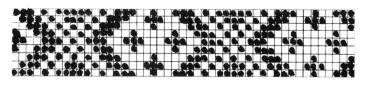

10c

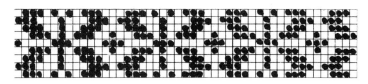

10d

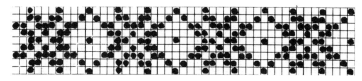

10e

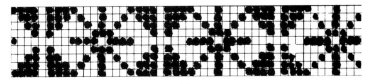

11a

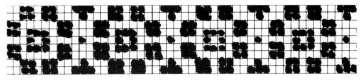

11b

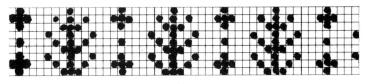

11c

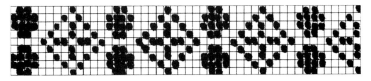

11d

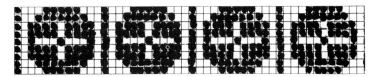

11e

10 & 11 Row Patterns

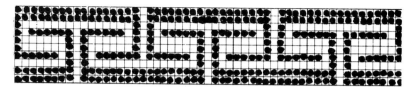

12a

12b

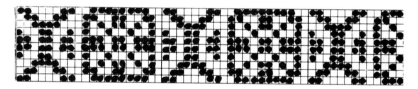

12c

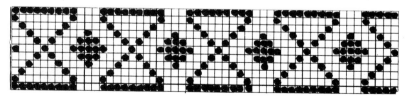

12d

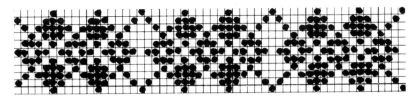

13a

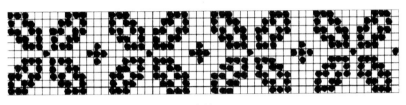

13b

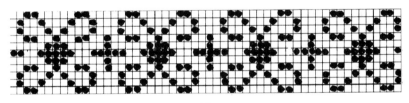

13c

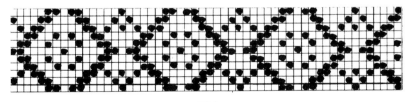

13d

10 & 11 Row Patterns *(continued)*

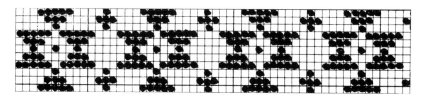

14a

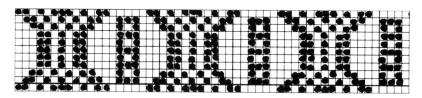

14b

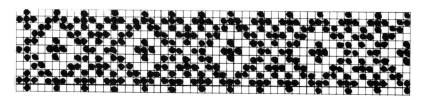

14c

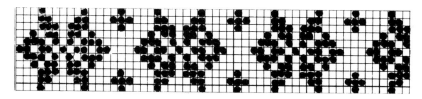

14d

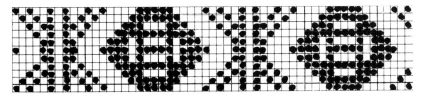

15a

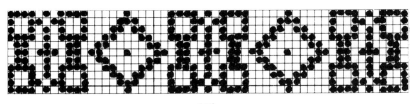

15b

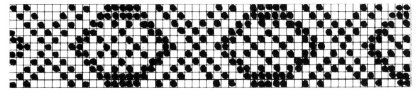

15c

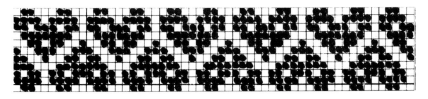

15d

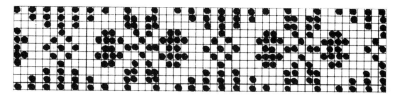

16a

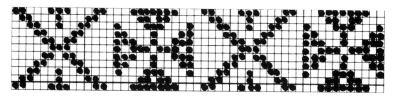

16b

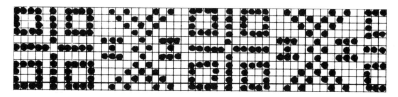

16c

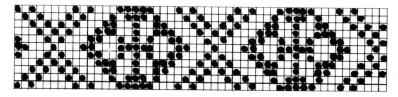

16d

10 & 11 Row Patterns *(continued)*

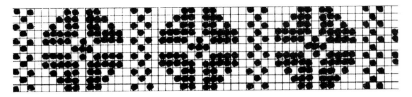

17a

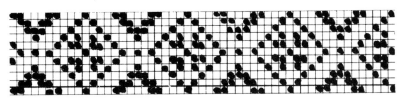

17b

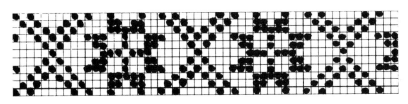

17c

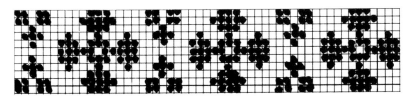

17d

13 Row Patterns

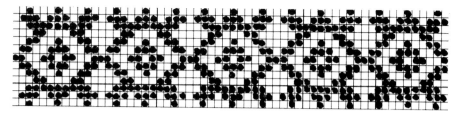

18a

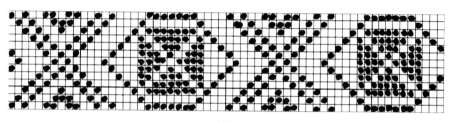

18b

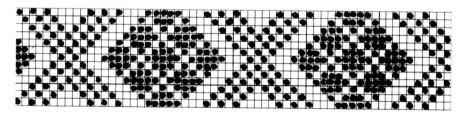

18c

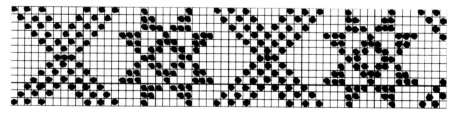

18d

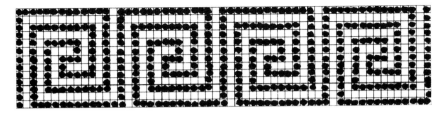

19a

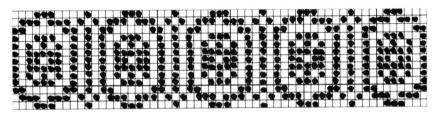

19b

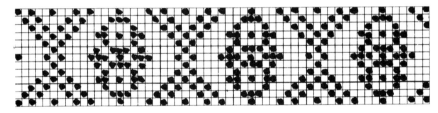

19c

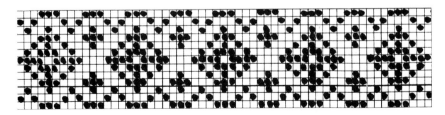

19d

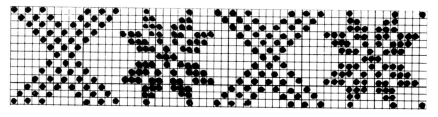

20a

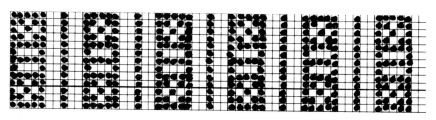

20b

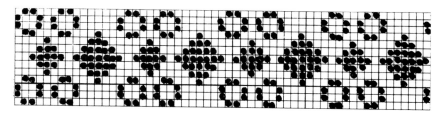

20c

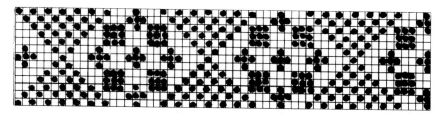

20d

13 Row Patterns *(continued)*

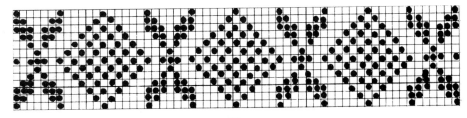

21a

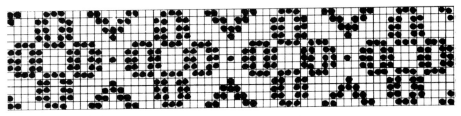

21b

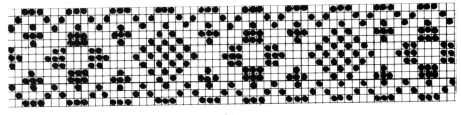

21c

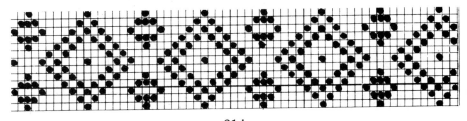

21d

36

15 Row Patterns

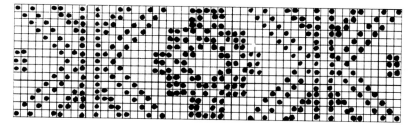

22a

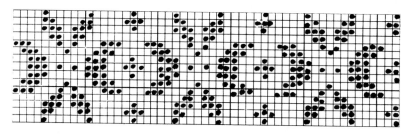

22b

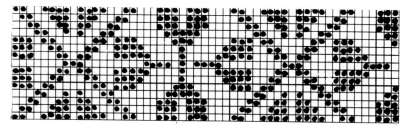

22c

37

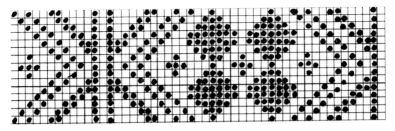

23a

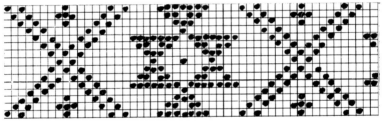

23b

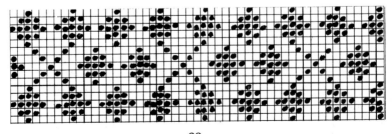

23c

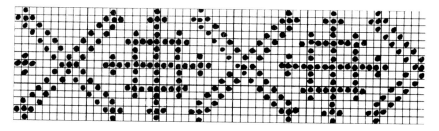

24a

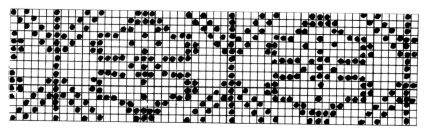

24b

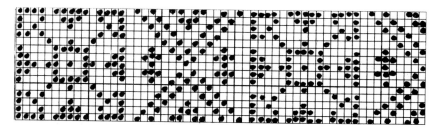

24c

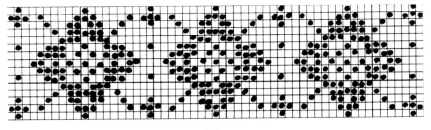

25a

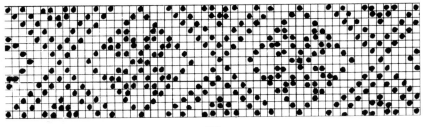

25b

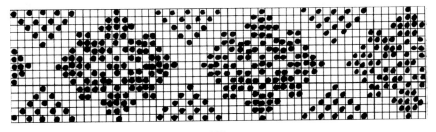

25c

17 Row Patterns

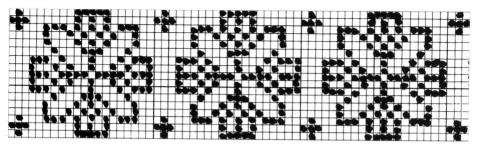

26a

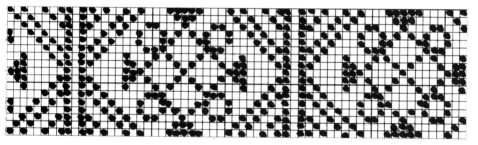

26b

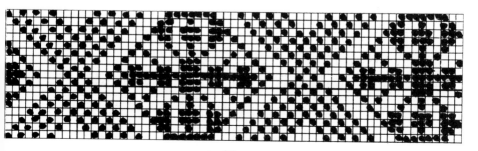

26c

41

17 Row Patterns *(continued)*

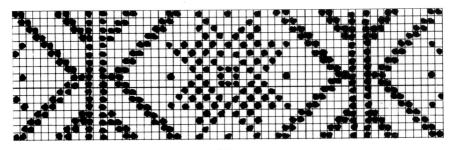

27a

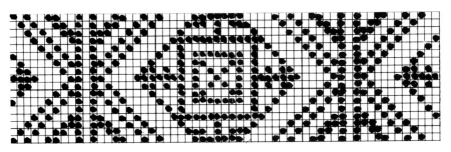

27b

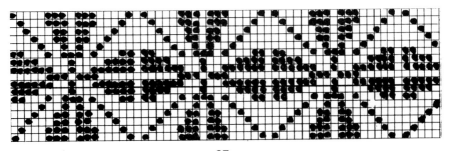

27c

42

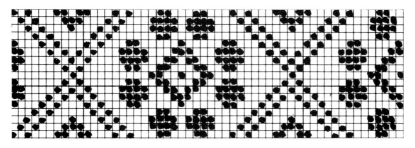

28a

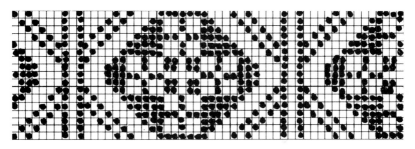

28b

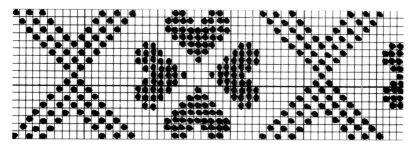

28c

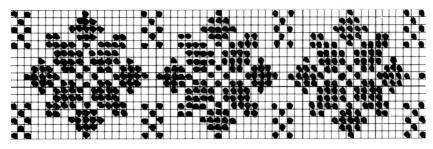

29a

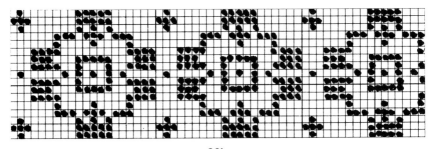

29b

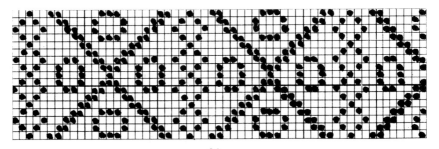

29c

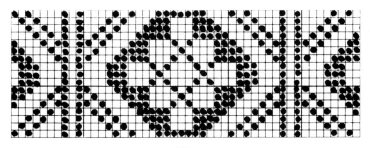

30a

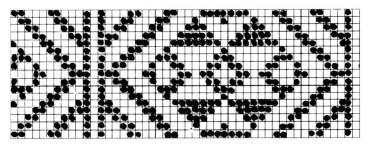

30b

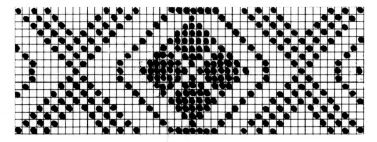

30c

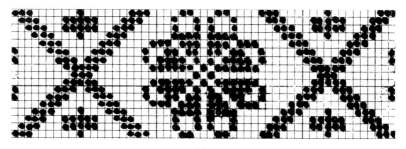

31a

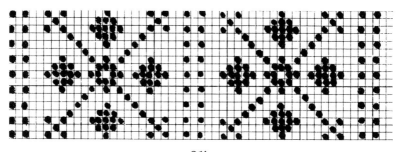

31b

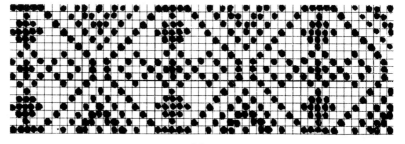

31c

19 & 21 Row Patterns

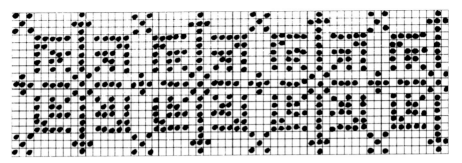

32a

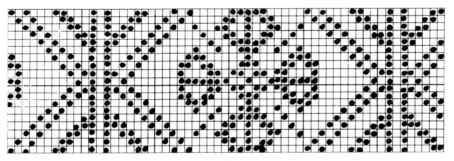

32b

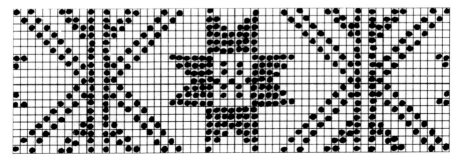

32c

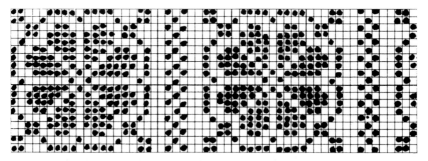

33a

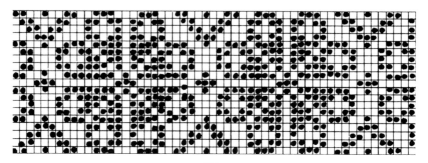

33b

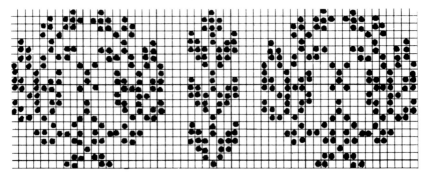

33c

Norwegian Stars

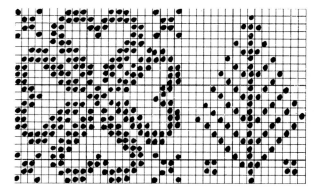

34a

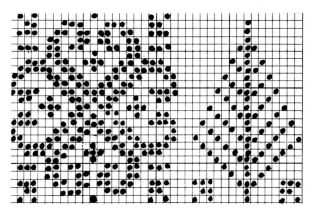

34b

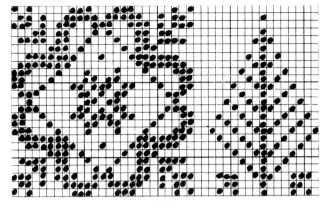

35a

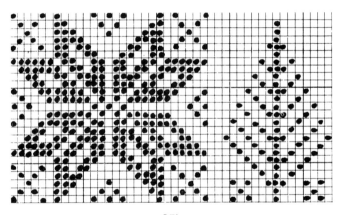

35b

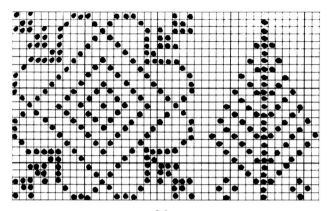

36a

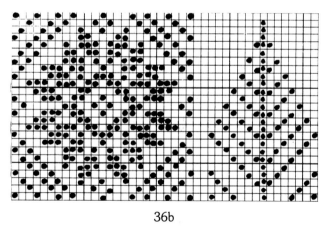

36b

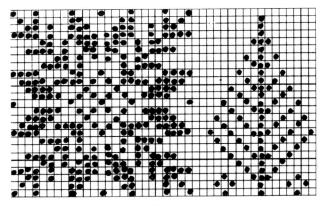

37a

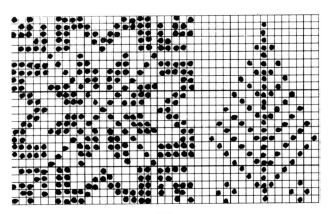

37b

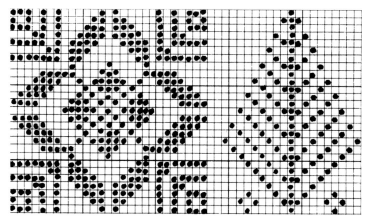

38a

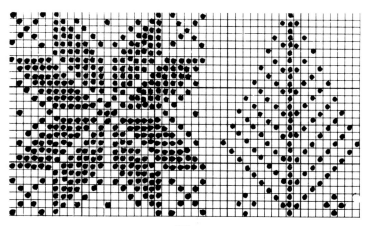

38b

Novelty Patterns

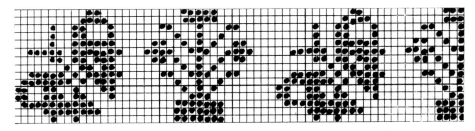

39a

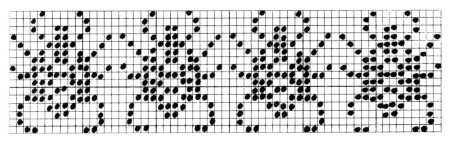

39b

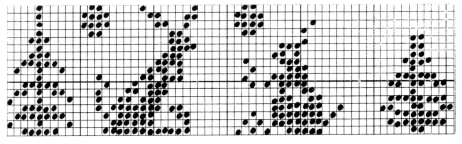

39c

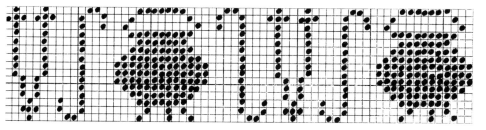

40a

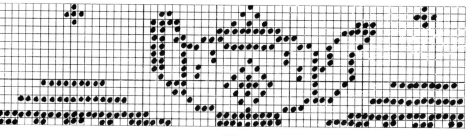

40b

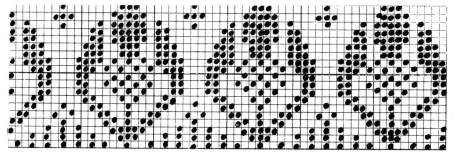

40c

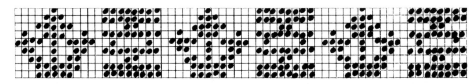

41a

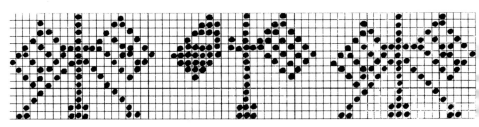

41b

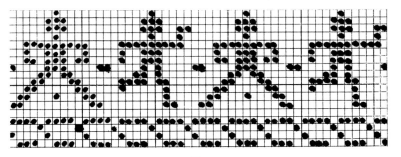

41c

All-Over Patterns

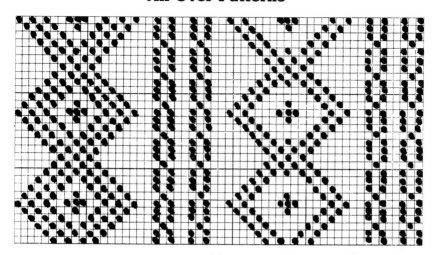

42a

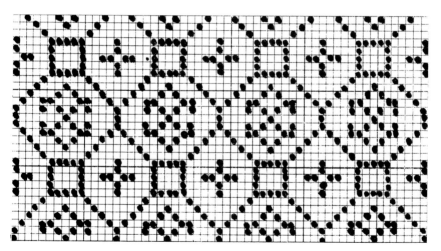

42b

43a

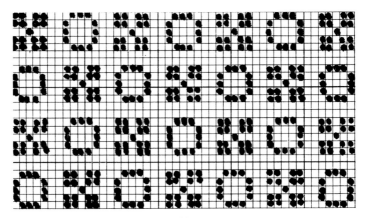

43b

NOTES

NOTES

NOTES

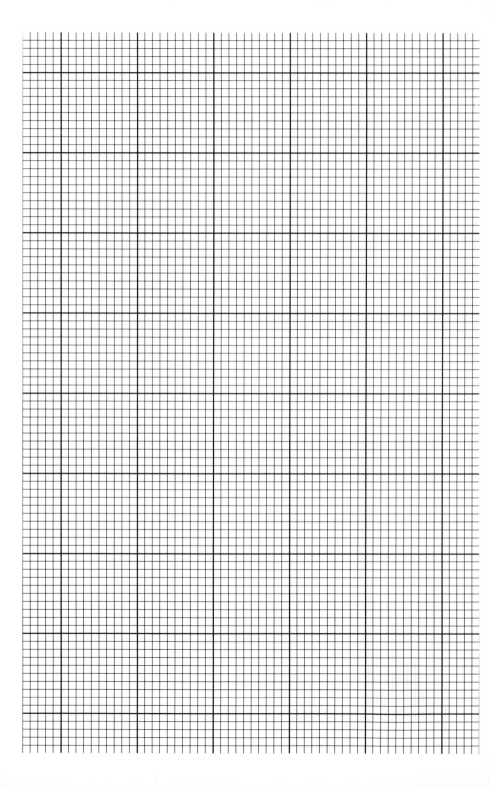

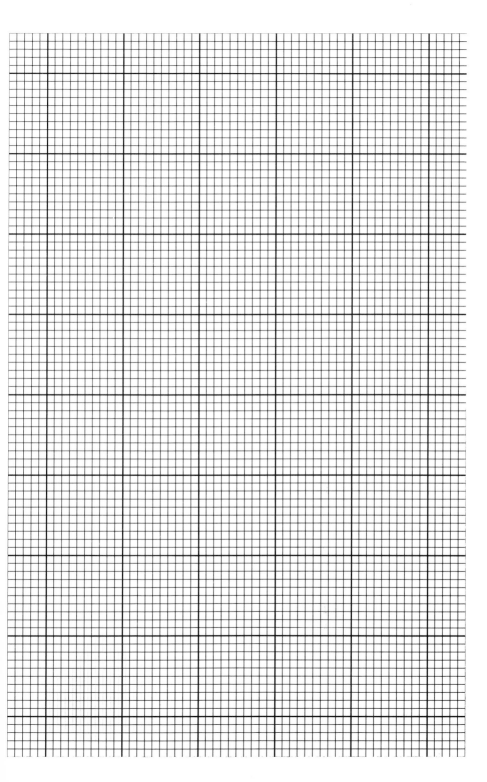

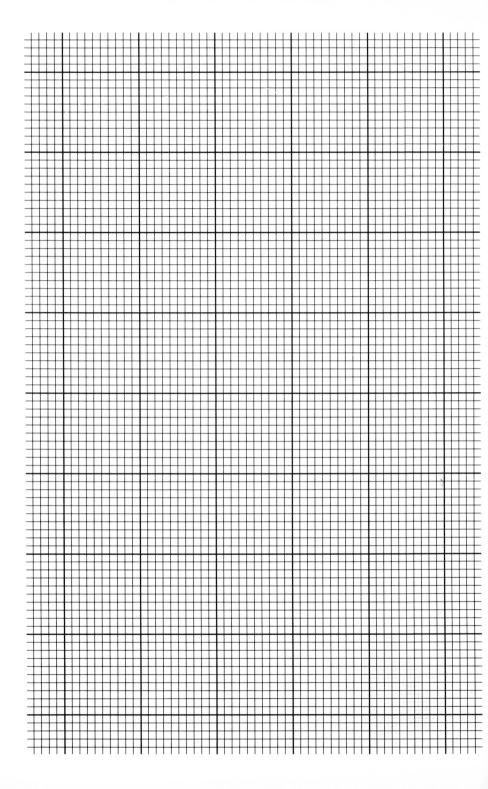

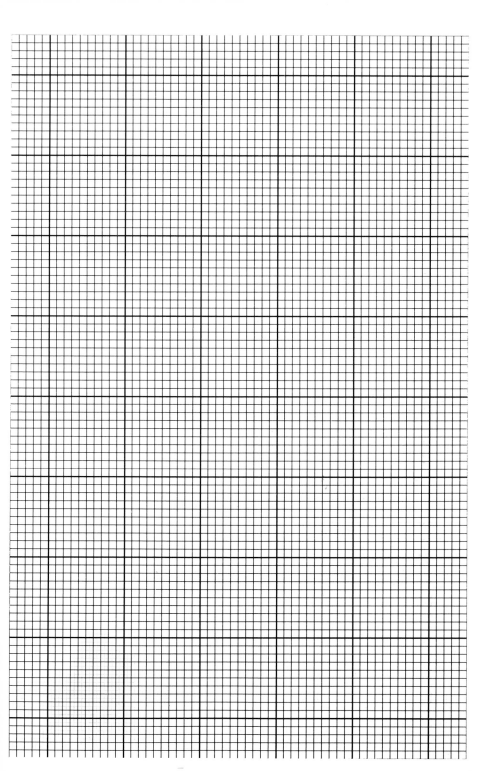